CLB 1365
Published in Great Britain 1985 by Crown Books.
Crown Books is a registered imprint of Colour Library Books Ltd.
© 1985 Illustrations and text: Colour Library Books Ltd.,
    Guildford, Surrey, England.
Filmsetting by Acesetters Ltd., Richmond, Surrey, England.
Produced by AGSA, in Barcelona, Spain.
Printed and bound in Barcelona, Spain by Rieusset and Eurobinder.
ISBN 0 86283 324 8
- Dep. Leg. B-10.238-85

SCOTLAND
FROM THE AIR

CROWN BOOKS

Previous pages: the small, neat fishing village of St Monance on the Firth of Forth is one of many such close-knit communities on the east coast, dependent for their livelihood on the often hostile sea.

These pages: Sir Walter Scott's country house at Abbotsford, his last and most famous home, stands on the banks of his beloved River Tweed. Built between 1817 and 1824, the house was designed largely by Scott himself. The writer's study has been preserved as he left it, and his impressive library contains some 20,000 rare books.

Overleaf: Culzean Castle, on the Strathclyde coast, is a typical product of the 18th century Picturesque style – a building of Georgian symmetry and order, but with medieval trimmings. Towers and turrets, battlements and machicolations are combined with sash windows and Robert Adam's characteristic arched recesses in his favoured Palladian tradition. Before its renovation the house was known simply as 'The Cove', but finding that a grandson of the first owner of the castle, John Kennedy, had styled himself 'Johannes Kennedy de Culzane' in 1492, Adam's patron wrote it 'Culzean' in the parish records, and 'Culzean' it became.

Dumfries (previous pages) is a
Royal Burgh on the River Nith,
situated opposite its sister town
of Maxwelltown on the far bank.
Dumfries is rich in historical
relics: the house where Robert
Burns died still stands, as does
the mausoleum in which he is
interred. The many-arched, 15th
century bridge is still used by
pedestrians, and a plaque in
Bridge Street marks the place
where the Red Comyn was
stabbed by Robert the Bruce in
1306.

These pages: winter light on
Glen Etive in the Grampian
Mountains of Strathclyde,
where the valley's many tarns
gather and flow to the sea
through the long arm of Loch
Etive.

Overleaf: winter's icy grip holds
Loch Morlich and the snow-clad
heights of the Cairngorms
beyond.

Previous pages: Kelvingrove
Park in Glasgow, where stands
the imposing Gothic fantasy of
the Art Gallery and Museum.
These were opened in 1901, and
the galleries contain one of the
finest municipal collections in
Britain.

These pages: the famous
landmark of Bass Rock rises
350 feet from the sea north-east
of North Berwick. There are
traces of old fortifications and of
a chapel on the island, though
now it holds only a lighthouse,
and large, noisy colonies of
seabirds.

Overleaf: broad and stately
Princes Street, Edinburgh's
most famous avenue, was
named in honour of the sons of
George III. The Street is lined
on the north side by a
distinguished array of shops,
clubs and hotels, while on the
south side the beautifully-tended
Princes Street Gardens drop
steeply away into what were the
depths of the Nor' Loch,
drained in 1760. The gardens
provide a setting for the 200ft-
high Scott Monument, the
Scottish-American War
Memorial, and the Floral Clock
of 1903, and beyond them rises
the guardian bastion of the
Castle.

Previous pages: the Royal Mile connects Edinburgh Castle with the sovereign's 16th century Palace of Holyroodhouse. Construction of the palace was begun in about 1500 by James IV, when he enlarged an existing guesthouse of Holyrood Abbey. The Abbey was founded as a Chapel Royal in 1128 by David I. According to legend, the King went hunting on a holy day, and was attacked by a stag. About to be gored, he seized the stag's antlers, and the animal vanished, leaving in the King's hand a Holy Cross or Rood. The Abbey was, supposedly, built on the spot where the miracle took place, and was for centuries the burial-place of Scottish kings and queens.

The great estuary of the Forth was for many years a barrier to communications in lowland Scotland, separating as it does two of its more populous regions. In the 1880s the great engineering feat of bridging the firth was undertaken by Sir John Fowler and Sir Benjamin Baker, and the mighty, cantilevered railway bridge (overleaf) was completed in 1890. The main spans are 1,710 feet across, and stand 150 feet above the water. The New Forth Bridge of 1964 (these pages), a suspension road bridge, finally replaced the ferry service which had traversed the waters for 800 years.

Previous pages: Scone Palace,
near Perth, is an early 19th-
century castellated building
occupying the site of the
Coronation Abbey of Scottish
kings. Here rested the
celebrated Stone of Scone –
traditionally identified with the
Stone of Destiny at Tara in
Ireland, which is said to have
been Jacob's pillow at Bethel –
until it was removed by the
English King Edward I in 1297,
and placed beneath the
Coronation Chair in
Westminster Abbey.

These pages: the Royal Burgh
of Dundee, on the Forth of Tay,
now operates considerable light
industry to supplement its old
staple industries of jute
production and jam making.
The jute industry began as a by-
product of the whaling industry,
which supplied oil for the city's
lamps in the 18th century.
Whale oil was mixed with raw
jute imported from India, which
could be woven into an
extremely versatile coarse
material. Mrs Keiller began
making the famous Dundee
marmalade in 1797, and the
fertile Carse of Gowrie to the
north-east now produces the
fruit used in the city's jam
industry.

Overleaf: the fine city of Perth
was created a Royal Burgh as
early as 1210, and was Scotland's
capital for a hundred years until
1437. In that year King James I
was murdered at the former
Blackfriar's Monastery, despite
the heroic attempts of Catherine
Douglas – a lady of the Queen –
to keep the murderers out by
placing her arm across the door
in place of a bar. The King's
widow and her young son,
James II, moved the court, and
hence the capital, to Edinburgh.

Previous pages: dark
Schiehallion rises for 3,547 feet
above Loch Rannoch, and is
one of the best known
landmarks of the Central
Highlands.

These pages: the barren moors
between Auchterarder and
Strath Earn have a name which
has made them well-known
throughout the golfing world:
Gleneagles. The golf courses
which lie beside the Gleneagles
Hotel are for many the Mecca
of the Royal and Ancient Game,
and are among the most famous
in the world.

Overleaf: built by Vanbrugh in
1718, Floors Castle lies near the
River Tweed in the hills of the
Border Region. The house
boasts 365 windows, and stands
in a beautiful, landscaped park.
A holly tree in the park
reputedly marks the place
where James II was killed by a
bursting cannon during his siege
of the castle which stood on this
site in 1460.

Loch Ness extends from south of Inverness to Fort Augustus (previous pages) where the Caledonian Canal empties into the loch. Stories of a monster in Loch Ness began at least as early as the 7th century, when St Adamnan, Abbot of Iona, wrote his biography of St Columba. In this he tells of that good man preventing a River Ness water monster from consuming a Pict in 565. Gaelic folklore says that the monster is an 'each visge', or fearsome water horse, one of which occupies every dark sheet of water in the Highlands.

The 15-mile-long island of Bute (these pages) nestles at the foot of the hilly Cowal peninsula, from which it is separated by a beautiful stretch of water known as the Kyles of Bute. Cattle used to be made to swim across this channel from Colintraive on the mainland to Rhubodach on Bute; now a car ferry makes the crossing.

Overleaf: Inverness, the beautifully situated 'Capital of the Highlands', lies on the River Ness at the north-east end of Glen More and the Caledonian canal. The strategic importance of the site has long been recognised, as witness the military installations, including a royal castle of 1141, a Cromwellian fortress of 1642 and two great military roads built after the Jacobite rebellion of 1745.

Previous pages and these pages: in the Royal Burgh of Pittenweem in Fifeshire old, red-roofed houses are grouped neatly around the ancient fishing harbour. Incorporated in the parsonage are traces of the Augustinian priory which was founded here in 1141.

When first mentioned in 1484, Balmoral Castle, was known as Bouchmorale, which is Gaelic for 'majestic dwelling'. It lies on a curve of the river in Royal Deeside, in the district of Mar, and was bought in 1852 by the Prince Consort as a Highland home for his royal wife. Queen Victoria later added Ballochbuie Forest to the property. The Castle has remained an occasional royal home ever since, with the Royal Family attending the nearby Braemar Games each summer.

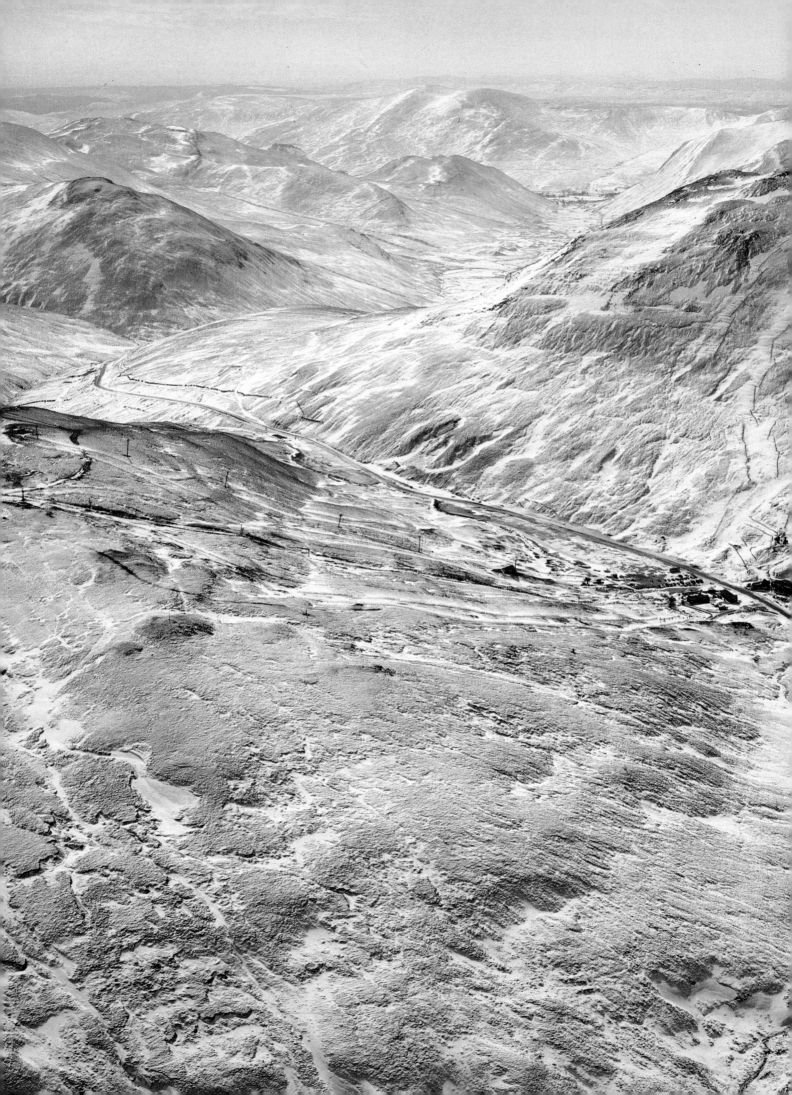

On purchasing Balmoral (previous pages) for £31,000, Prince Albert had the castle rebuilt in his own elaborate version of the Scottish Baronial style. The resultant chateau-like mansion was first used as a royal residence in 1855, and is rich in 'fairy-tale' turrets and gables.

These pages: a wintry Glen Shee in the heart of the Grampians, where a fine road now links Blairgowrie and the South with Braemar on Royal Deeside.

The port of Tarbert in Strathclyde (overleaf) is the centre of the Loch Fyne herring industry. It lies on the tiny isthmus on the shores of East Loch Tarbert – a little neck of land linking Knapdale with Kintyre. Hills almost encircle Tarbert and its harbour, with Sliabh Gaoil rising 1,840 feet in the hills of South Knapdale to the north-west. In 1093 Magnus Barefoot of Norway is said to have been dragged by his warriors in a longship from Tarbert across the isthmus – a distance of nearly two miles.

Mull

Tobermory, or 'St Mary's Well', (previous pages) is the chief town on the Island of Mull. It was founded in 1788 by the Society for the Encouragement of the British Fisheries, but failed to realise the hopes of its founders, and has never been an important fishing station. It stands on the shores of a bay in which one of the galleons of the Spanish Armada was blown up and sunk in 1588 by Donald Glas Maclean, a Scottish hostage. Many unsuccessful attempts have since been made to find the galleon's supposed treasure.

Further south, the flat, green Isle of Gigha (these pages) is separated from the west coast of Kintyre by the Sound of Gigha. Beyond its rocky coast lie the hills of distant Islay, across the Sound of Jura.

Overleaf: the desolate beauty of South Harris in the Outer Hebrides. Here, at Kennacley, crofters use every available foot of fertile ground, and fish the surrounding seas.

Where the Tay meets the North Sea, the headland of Fife is edged with golden sands, and it is here, on the northern shore, that the Royal Burgh of St Andrews (following page) stands. Though for many the town holds associations only with the Royal and Ancient Game of golf, it was once the ecclesiastical centre for Scotland – its Cathedral now lies in ruins beside the quay – and boasts the country's oldest University, founded in 1412.